RAIN FOREST
REVEALED

Written by
JEN GREEN

LONDON, NEW YORK, MUNICH,
MELBOURNE, and DELHI

PROJECT EDITOR CLARE LISTER
SENIOR DESIGNERS JIM GREEN, BILL MASON
PHOTOSHOP ILLUSTRATOR MARK LONGWORTH
MANAGING ART EDITOR
SOPHIA M. TAMPAKOPOULOS TURNER
MANAGING EDITOR LINDA ESPOSITO
CATEGORY PUBLISHER SUE GRABHAM
ART DIRECTOR SIMON WEBB
PICTURE RESEARCHERS JO DE GRAY,
HARRIET MILLS
DTP DESIGNER SIU HO
PRODUCTION CONTROLLER
DULCIE ROWE

First American Edition, 2004

Published in the United States by
DK Publishing, Inc.
375 Hudson Street
New York, New York 10014

04 05 06 07 08 10 9 8 7 6 5 4 3 2 1

Library of Congress Cataloging-in-Publication Data
Green, Jen.
Rain forest / written by Jen Green.-- 1st American ed.
p. cm. -- (DK revealed)
ISBN 0-7566-0538-5 (plcj)
1. Rain forest--Juvenile literature. 2. Toy and movable books--
Specimens. I. Title. II. Series.
QH86.G72 2004
578.734--dc22
2004008660
ISBN 0-7566-0538-5

Color reproduction by Colourscan, Singapore

Printed in China by Leo Paper Products

Discover more at
www.dk.com

CONTENTS

GREEN WORLDS

LUSH RAIN FORESTS ARE RICH HABITATS, home to more living things than anywhere else on Earth. These warm, moist forests are special places, where huge trees soar upward to create a dense platform of leaves overhead. Colorful birds and agile monkeys flit through the branches, and eerie calls pierce the air. Rain forests grow in wet areas that receive more than 78 in (200 cm) of rain annually. They are important because they help regulate Earth's climate, recycling moisture and keeping temperatures even. Scientists identify many different types of rain forests, including tropical and temperate rain forests, cloud forests, flooded forests, and mangrove swamps.

Emergent layer

Canopy

Understory

Forest floor

STORIES
Scientists divide forests into four vertical layers called stories. Trees and plants root on the floor. Branchless tree trunks shoot up through the understory. Trees unfurl their leaves high in the air, forming the canopy. Tall trees called emergents grow above the canopy to make the top layer.

FORESTS OF THE WORLD
Most tropical forests (shown in green above) are located in a narrow band, within 10 degrees of the equator. Today, rain forests cover under 6 percent of Earth's land surface.

FLOODED TEMPERATE FOREST
In rain forests, drenching rain falls daily. The water drains away to form mighty rivers, and bordering low-lying land is regularly flooded. Temperate forests, such as this one in northwestern US, are cooler than tropical forests, and have greater seasonal variation.

CLOUD FOREST

Montane forests grow on hills and mountains. They are also called cloud forests because the trees here are usually swathed in mist. Moisture-loving mosses and ferns coat the boughs in this saturated environment. Trees grow shorter at high altitudes.

TROPICAL RAIN FOREST

Lying close to the equator, tropical forests are hot and wet all year round, with average temperatures of around 77°F (27°C). These are ideal growing conditions for plants. With little seasonal variation, the trees keep their leaves and can flower at any time of year.

PLANT DIVERSITY

Rain forests are home to an incredible two-thirds of the world's flowering plant species. In addition to flowering plants, such as this orchid, many tree species and nonflowering plants also thrive here, including ferns and vines.

The orchid's sweet nectar attracts bees.

MANGROVE SWAMPS

With their roots jutting out of the thick river silt, mangrove trees line the moist coasts and river estuaries of the tropics. The mud and saltwater are low in oxygen, so the trees breathe with the help of knobbly, arching roots called pneumatophores. These take in oxygen through large pores (holes) called lenticles.

ANIMAL LIFE

Rain forests support a huge variety of animals, from large mammals such as this jaguar to birds, reptiles, amphibians, and countless insects. Some experts estimate that only one-tenth of the species found in rain forests have been identified.

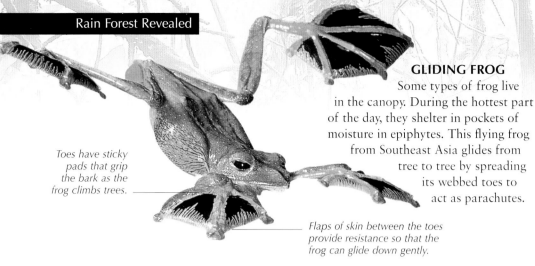

GLIDING FROG
Some types of frog live in the canopy. During the hottest part of the day, they shelter in pockets of moisture in epiphytes. This flying frog from Southeast Asia glides from tree to tree by spreading its webbed toes to act as parachutes.

Toes have sticky pads that grip the bark as the frog climbs trees.

Flaps of skin between the toes provide resistance so that the frog can glide down gently.

IN THE TREETOPS

RAIN FOREST TREES SPREAD THEIR BRANCHES to form a dense, interlocking mass of leaves called the canopy, some 100–130 ft (30–45 m) off the ground. Most living things in rain forests inhabit this leafy layer. Conditions in the topmost trees are extreme—branches are tossed in high winds, drenched by heavy rain, and scorched in the sunshine. The lower canopy is more sheltered. Life here includes plants called epiphytes, which root high on tree branches, and animals that are either expert fliers or strong climbers.

DRIP TIPS
Torrential rain falls most afternoons in tropical forests. Many trees have leaves that narrow to slender points known as drip tips, which shed excess moisture. This helps to prevent the leaves from becoming waterlogged, and stops tiny plants called algae from coating the surface and harming the tree.

NUT-CRACKING PARROT
South American macaws are among the most colorful birds of the upper canopy. Their short wings make it easier for them to steer between branches as they search for fruit. The macaw's powerful hooked bill works like a nutcracker, breaking open tough-shelled seeds.

Macaws have short wings to fly between the leaves in the dense canopy.

Poison arrow frog

Water collects in the ring of leaves.

Flatworm

Tree branch

AIR PLANTS
Epiphytes (also called air plants) do not steal nourishment from the trees they grow on, but use them to reach the light. They obtain nourishment from air and water. This bromeliad is a type of epiphyte that catches water in its leaves.

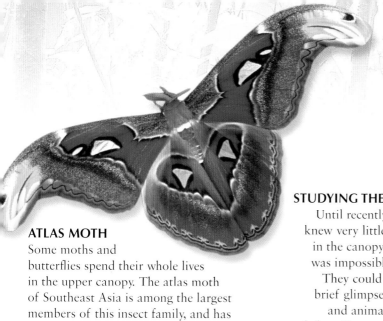

ATLAS MOTH

Some moths and
butterflies spend their whole lives
in the upper canopy. The atlas moth
of Southeast Asia is among the largest
members of this insect family, and has
a wingspan of 12 in (30 cm).

GREEN BLANKET

An unbroken blanket of green stretches to
the horizon in the world's largest tropical
forest, the Amazon rain forest in South
America. This huge forest covers 2.5 million
sq miles (6 million square km). Airplanes
can fly over forests like these, but the only
way to cross them at ground level is by
using rivers, which act as watery highways.

STUDYING THE CANOPY

Until recently, scientists
knew very little about life
in the canopy because it
was impossible to reach.
They could only catch
brief glimpses of plants
and animals from far
below. Now scientists can
carry out detailed studies
of canopy life using
aerial walkways, cranes,
and even hot-air balloons.

The squirrel monkey's tail can grow longer than its entire body.

SKILLFUL ACROBAT

The squirrel monkey has
a slim build. It can scamper
among flimsy branches in search of
fruit, nuts, insects, and birds' eggs. Its
mobile tail helps it to balance and even
acts as a fifth limb to grip boughs.

FOREST FLOOR

THE FLOOR OF THE RAIN FOREST teems with life, though many creatures are hidden. This minihabitat is like a tiny version of the world above, where living things depend on one another for food. Trees and plants draw nourishment from the soil, minibeasts feed on plants, and predators prey on weaker creatures. When animals and plants die, fungi, insects, and microscopic bacteria digest and break down their remains, releasing minerals into the soil to nourish more plants, and the cycle of life continues.

3

EXPLORING THE FOREST FLOOR

1 Bracket fungus: *it grows on a rotting tree, sending out a network of fibers that digest dead wood*

2 Cricket: *this solitary plant-eating insect is about to become the army ants' next victim*

3 Mushroom caps: *a network of cells called hyphae spread in the soil below the sprouting caps*

4 Rotting log: *millipedes and other plant-eating minibeasts, and also a predatory spider live inside*

5 Army ants: *these fierce, meat-eating insects march through forests, devouring everything in their path*

6 Leaf katydid: *the colors and patterns on this insect's wings fool predators*

7 Termite nest: *huge numbers of termites live together in a cooperative group called a colony*

8 Leaf-cutter ants: *the ants take leaves back to their nest to fertilize the fungi that they eat*

9 Pill millipedes: *the bugs roll into a ball to avoid attack from predators, such as army ants*

10 Rat carcass: *fly eggs laid on the rat's body hatch into maggots that feed on the dead rat's flesh*

ON THE GROUND

THE DENSE PLANT LIFE of the forest canopy acts like a leaky umbrella, shielding the layers below from light and moisture. Only a tiny fraction of the sunlight that bathes the treetops filters through to reach the forest floor, and rain can take up to 10 minutes to drip to the ground. The soil of tropical forests is surprisingly thin and poor because plants absorb all the nourishment. A thick carpet of fallen leaves and other rotting vegetation covers the ground, where plant-eating animals sift for food among the leaf litter and keep watch for lurking predators.

HIDDEN VIPER
The West African gaboon viper is a deadly predator. The colors and patterns on its skin camouflage (disguise) it among the dead leaves. It lies in wait for prey such as rodents, amphibians, and ground-dwelling birds. Its long fangs inject a venom that stops the prey's heartbeat and causes massive bleeding.

Each body segment (section) has one pair of legs.

Two long antennae help the centipede to detect food.

A bony ridge called a casque acts as a helmet as the bird crashes through thick undergrowth.

HARD-HEADED BIRD
Cassowaries are large flightless birds from the forests of Australia and New Guinea. These huge birds grow to 5 ft (1.5 m) and have little to fear as they wander the forest searching for fruit and seeds. Their large size deters most enemies, but if cornered, they can deliver a violent kick with their powerful, sharp-clawed feet. The bony crest on the bird's head gives further protection.

POISONOUS CENTIPEDE
Predators of the forest floor include minibeasts like this South American centipede. It can grow up to 8 in (20 cm) long. During the night, this many-legged hunter chases after prey, such as worms, slugs, and insects, which it stabs with poisoned fangs.

A SPLASH OF COLOR

Much of the forest floor is too dry and shady for plants to flourish. Heliconia and other colorful species bloom in sunny spots created by fallen trees. There are more than 450 different types of heliconia. They are also called lobster claws because of the shape of their flowers.

Buttress roots can begin 30 ft (9 m) or so up the trunk.

ZEBRA-STRIPED OKAPI

These shy, solitary mammals from West Africa were only discovered in 1901. The okapi's long tongue reaches up to rip blossoms, leaves, and buds from low branches.

The hooves have glands that secrete (give off) a scent to mark their territory.

BUTTRESS ROOTS

Tall forest trees anchor themselves in the shallow soil of rain forests with sideways-branching roots called buttress roots. These hard wings of wood spread outward from the lower trunk and resemble the buttresses that support buildings. Buttress roots also support trees in swampy ground, such as here on the Caribbean island of Trinidad.

13

THE SUSTAINING FOREST

R AIN FOREST TREES AND PLANTS sustain (support) not only
themselves, but countless other organisms (living things) too, both
within and outside the forest. Rooted in the soil, plants cannot move
around to find their food, as animals do. Instead, they make their own
food through an incredible process called photosynthesis.
A by-product of this process is oxygen, which animals
need to breathe. Rain forest plants also
help to keep surrounding regions moist
by recycling water. All the animals
of the rain forest depend on plants
for food directly or indirectly, as
they either eat plant matter
or prey on plant-eaters.

PHOTOSYNTHESIS

The green parts of a plant
contain a substance called
chlorophyll, which performs a
chemical reaction using energy
from sunlight. Chlorophyll
converts carbon dioxide
gas (from the air) and
water and minerals
drawn up by the roots
into a sugary food,
which the plant stores
as starch. Oxygen is
released as waste.

*The strangler fig forms
a network of roots
around the host tree.*

*This stoma (tiny
pore) on the leaf's
underside absorbs
carbon dioxide
and gives off
oxygen and water.*

KILLER PLANT

The strangler fig sprouts high
on another forest tree from a
seed dropped by a bird. It
sends down roots that spread
through the soil to take the
host tree's moisture. The fig's
growth forms a tight corset
around the host and strangles
it. The host tree dies, leaving
the fig standing like an empty
cage, seen here from below.

SEED MEDICINE
Some rain forest plants contain chemicals that local people have used as medicine for centuries. Scientists have discovered that the seeds of the Moreton Bay chestnut from Australia contain a chemical called castanospermine that can be used to combat certain disease-causing viruses, including the HIV virus that causes AIDS.

ROOT SYSTEMS
The roots of mighty trees form extensive networks both below and above ground. When seedlings sprout high on trees or buildings, they send down roots that eventually form huge woody growths. This tree has taken root over the ruins of the ancient temple of Angkor Wat in Cambodia, Southeast Asia.

TEMPERATE GIANT
This huge, thick-trunked tree is a kauri pine from the temperate forest of New Zealand. Mature kauri pines have extensive branches, which provide habitats for a wide range of plants, especially epiphytes.

WATER FALL
Rain forest trees work like sponges, soaking up rainfall that would otherwise drain off into rivers. The trees draw up water through their roots, use it for growth, and release the excess through their leaves as water vapor. Droplets of water vapor form clouds, which shed their rain back on the forest, and so water is constantly recycled to sustain life.

INSECT TRAP

THE DEADLY NEPENTHES pitcher plant thrives in the wet, boggy rain forests of Madagascar. It does not get all its nutrients from the ground like most plants, because the soil it grows in is poor. So, it relies on another way to get extra nutrients. Insects are lured to the plant by the tempting scent it exudes and the beautiful reds and yellows of its pitchers. It may seem enticing, but it is a death trap for minibeasts. Insects land on the slippery rim, lose their footing, and slide helplessly down into a lethal stew of enzymes and bacteria and are slowly digested.

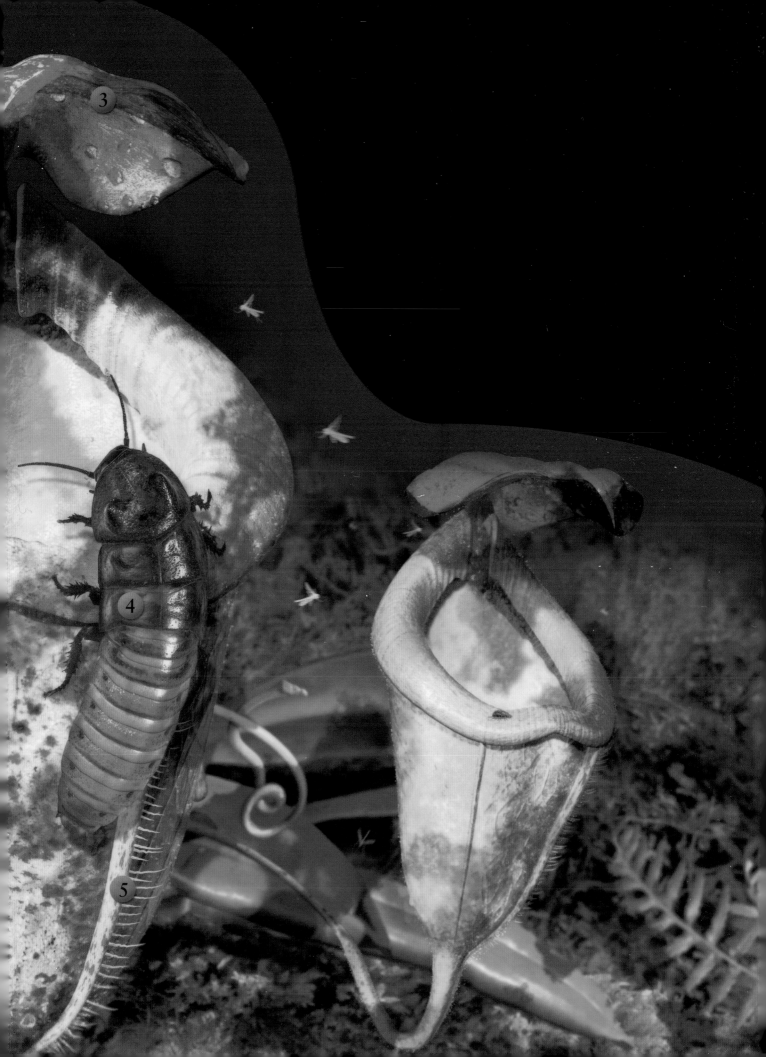

EXPLORING A NEPENTHES PITCHER PLANT

1. **Peristome:** *the slippery rim of the pitcher entices insects by producing a lot of nectar*

2. **Inside walls:** *sticky, downward-pointing hairs stop insects from climbing out*

3. **Lid:** *stops rainwater from entering the pitcher and diluting the contents*

4. **Giant hissing cockroach:** *a cockroach is attracted by the nectar and climbs on to the rim*

5. **Spiny wings:** *the outer surface of the pitcher has ridges that guide insects up to the rim*

6. **New habitat:** *The lid shrivels as a pitcher dies. It fills with rainwater, creating a microhabitat where frogs lay eggs*

7. **Digestive juices:** *movement inside the pitcher causes digestive glands to release enzymes to digest its prey*

8. **Crab spider:** *a spider that has adapted to balance on the pitcher's rim, where it hunts prey*

9. **Baby pitcher:** *the plant sprouts new pitchers, which grow up to 8 in (20 cm) long*

10. **Stem:** *the plant's long stalks deliver nutrients from the digested insects to the rest of the plant*

An aracari's long beak can reach fruit dangling from thin branches that would not support its weight.

SETTING SEED

M OST RAIN FOREST PLANTS reproduce by making seeds. To do this a plant's flowers must first be fertilized by pollen from another plant of the same type. This is called pollination. Plants rely on various means to transfer pollen from one plant to another. Some pollen is carried by the wind, but most pollen is transported by insects, bats, and birds. Plants attract the animals by offering a reward of sugary nectar. Their flowers advertise the nectar with sweet scents or bright colors. Once fertilized, seeds grow inside fruits, nuts, or cones. Seeds must be scattered far and wide, so that young plants do not compete with their parents for light and water.

NUT-EATER
Some plant seeds develop inside the tough outer case of nuts. Animals such as toucans and aracaris crack open the nuts and eat the seeds. The seeds are later deposited in another part of the forest in the animal's droppings.

GERMINATION
Seeds germinate (sprout) when conditions are favorable, either on the forest floor or high in the canopy on surfaces such as palm fronds, as here. In light, moist conditions, the seed case splits open. First, a tiny root emerges and grows downward, then a green shoot appears and rises upward.

TEMPTING FRUIT
Many plants bribe animals to carry their seeds by offering food in the form of juicy fruits and berries. The fruits of the unusual *Tamia Muya* tree from the Amazon rain forest sprout from buds on the trunk, not on slender branches as with most trees.

BLOWING IN THE WIND

Few rain forest trees use the wind to spread their seeds, because there are not many air currents in the sheltered canopy. Kapok trees are tall emergents that rise above the canopy, where breezes can disperse their seeds. Their seed pods split open to reveal ripe seeds surrounded by a fluffy coating, which wafts away on the wind.

BAT-POLLINATED BLOSSOMS

Many plants use flying creatures such as bats to carry their pollen. This bat is feeding on the nectar of banksia, which grows in Australasian rain forests. Dusty pollen clings to the bat's fur and then drops off to fertilize the next plant it visits.

SMELLY PLANTS

Southeast Asian rafflesias are the world's largest flowers, measuring 3 ft (1 m) across. The flowers release a strong stench, like rotting meat, to attract the insects that pollinate the plant.

The plant releases a sweet scent at night to attract bats.

The silverback gorilla develops silver-gray hair at about 11 or 12 years old.

A seedling sprouts in fertile silt by the river.

FLOATING SEEDS

Some rain forest plants that grow near water produce floating seeds, encased by a tough, waterproof nut with a cork- or air-filled layer that makes them buoyant (float). The ripe seeds drop into the water and are carried away by the current.

GORILLA FOOD

Juicy nuts and berries are a prized food source for many rain forest animals, including this African gorilla. Many animals carry their finds to a safe spot where they can feed in peace, which helps seeds to germinate away from the parent plant.

FOREST FOOD WEB

ALL LIVING THINGS IN THE RAIN FOREST ecosystem depend on one another for food and are linked in a complex web of life. Plants, which use sunlight energy to make their own food, form the base of the food chain. Next come herbivores (plant-eaters), which feed on the leaves, flowers, fruits, seeds, or bark of plants. At the top of the chain are carnivores (meat-eaters), which feed on herbivores as well as any weaker carnivores. Fungi and other decomposers form a vital link in forest food webs. By feeding on dead plants and animals, they assist the rotting process, which returns nutrients to the soil to promote more plant growth.

SMALL PREY
Caterpillars are herbivores. They eat huge quantities of plant matter to get the energy they need to mature. Being wingless, caterpillars make easy prey for predators such as birds.

TOP PREDATOR
Jaguars are the biggest cats of the Amazon rain forest. These expert climbers and swimmers use strength and cunning to hunt a wide range of prey, from otters to armadillos. Top predators like jaguars are often scarce because large numbers of prey are needed to feed them.

INSECT-EATER
Banded pittas from Southeast Asia use their sharp eyesight and sense of smell to track prey on the ground. They thrive on a diet of invertebrates (creatures without backbones), including snails, worms, and insects. In turn, pittas are food for larger predators.

BLOOD-THIRSTY VAMPIRE

Vampire bats are parasites (animals that feed on other creatures without killing them). These night-active mammals suck other animals' blood. The bat creeps up quietly on its victim and pierces the animal's skin with its fangs without disturbing it.

The bat's fangs are razor-sharp canine teeth at the front of its mouth.

Sharp claws help the bat to scramble up the slippery hair of victims.

PARASITIC PLANT

Plants can also live as parasites. The dodder plant's cells do not have chlorophyll, so it cannot make its own food. The dodder infests the stems of other plants. The parasite germinates from a seed that lodges in the host plant's stem, where it taps into the host cell's tissues to steal food.

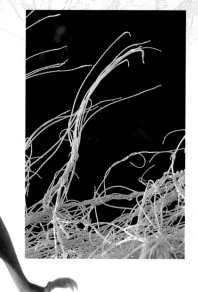

Gills on the underside of the mushroom caps release spores.

UNFUSSY MANDRILL

Animals that eat both plants and animals are called omnivores. The primate family, which includes apes, monkeys, and humans, has many examples. Mandrills are the largest forest-dwelling monkeys. They mainly eat fruits, nuts, and leaves, but they also catch invertebrates and even small vertebrates (backboned animals).

RECYCLING FUNGI

Fungi are not plants but a different group of living things. The main part of the fungus is a network of threadlike cells below ground. These cells take nutrients from rotting plants. When the fungus is ready to reproduce, it grows fruiting mushroom caps above ground. The caps release reproductive cells called spores that drift away on the wind.

Bright colors and striking markings on the male mandrill's face are designed to attract the opposite sex.

WATER WORLD

THE MIGHTY AMAZON RIVER dominates the Amazon rain forest. The gushing waters flow 4,000 miles (6,450 km) from the Andes to the Atlantic. Low-lying land by the river floods during the rainy season (from March to August), and plants spend up to six months of the year underwater. During the dry season, the forest floor and understory are home to land animals such as tapirs and jaguars. When the rains come the scene is transformed. Fish, caimans, and river dolphins search for food among the submerged roots.

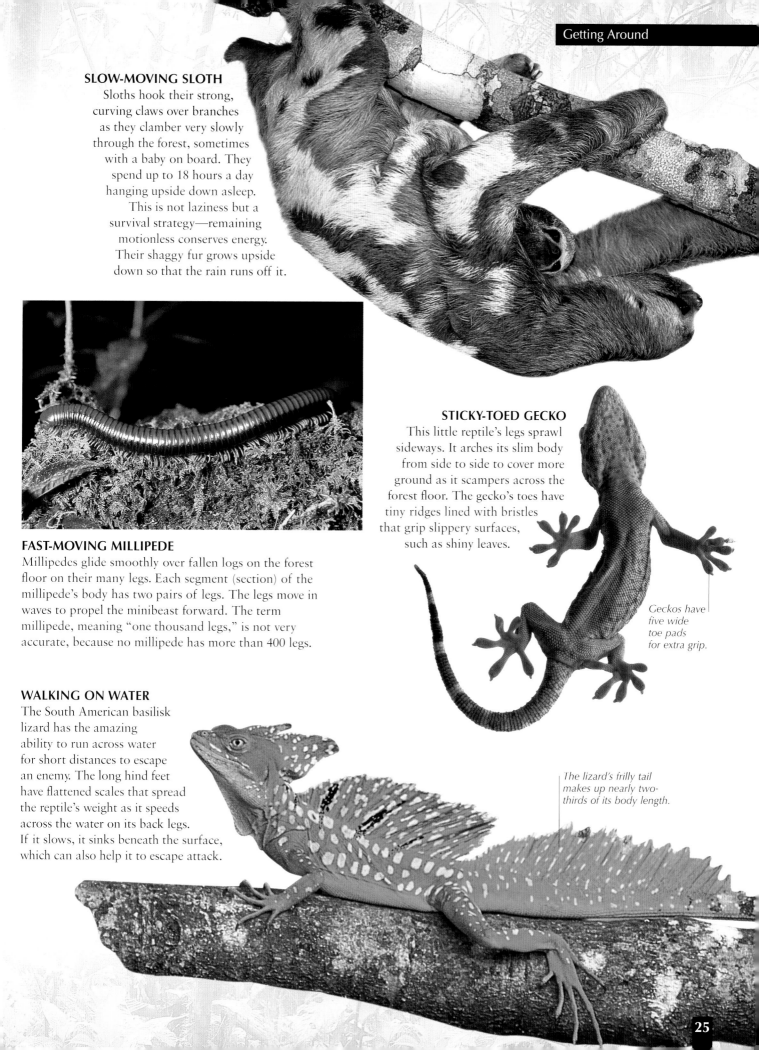

SLOW-MOVING SLOTH

Sloths hook their strong, curving claws over branches as they clamber very slowly through the forest, sometimes with a baby on board. They spend up to 18 hours a day hanging upside down asleep. This is not laziness but a survival strategy—remaining motionless conserves energy. Their shaggy fur grows upside down so that the rain runs off it.

FAST-MOVING MILLIPEDE

Millipedes glide smoothly over fallen logs on the forest floor on their many legs. Each segment (section) of the millipede's body has two pairs of legs. The legs move in waves to propel the minibeast forward. The term millipede, meaning "one thousand legs," is not very accurate, because no millipede has more than 400 legs.

STICKY-TOED GECKO

This little reptile's legs sprawl sideways. It arches its slim body from side to side to cover more ground as it scampers across the forest floor. The gecko's toes have tiny ridges lined with bristles that grip slippery surfaces, such as shiny leaves.

Geckos have five wide toe pads for extra grip.

WALKING ON WATER

The South American basilisk lizard has the amazing ability to run across water for short distances to escape an enemy. The long hind feet have flattened scales that spread the reptile's weight as it speeds across the water on its back legs. If it slows, it sinks beneath the surface, which can also help it to escape attack.

The lizard's frilly tail makes up nearly two-thirds of its body length.

25

CONSTANT DANGER

RAIN FORESTS ARE PERILOUS places, where the rule is eat, or be eaten. Plant-eating animals face a daily struggle to find food, while avoiding capture by predators. Meanwhile, predators use their keen senses to locate victims. They must then get close enough to use teeth, claws, or other weapons to catch, overpower, and kill their prey. Many animals can approach prey without being noticed or hide from predators by using camouflage—their colors and patterns help them blend with the background. However, some creatures that are poisonous use a different tactic. They have bright colors that serve as a warning that they should be left alone. Other creatures mimic the colors of a poisonous animal to put off potential predators.

STRANGLEHOLD
The boa constrictor kills by squeezing prey to death. It wraps itself around its victim and tightens its grip as the animal breathes out, leaving it no space to breathe in again.

CAMOUFLAGE EXPERT
Chameleons use camouflage both to sneak up on their prey and to avoid predators. They can change their body color to match their surroundings. The hunting chameleon creeps within range and then shoots out its long, sticky tongue at lightning speed to capture its insect prey.

The chameleon changes color by spreading or contracting grains of pigment in its skin.

FOREST PROWLER
Pumas, also known as cougars and mountain lions, are stealthy predators of South American rain forests. Most individuals are tawny-colored, but some are jet-black. These killers mainly hunt mammals, from small rodents to deer and cattle. The solitary stalker creeps up on its prey, crouching low to avoid detection. Then it lunges forward and kills its victim with a bite to the neck.

BRIGHT WARNING

The skin of poison arrow frogs has a very strong poison. Instead of hiding from potential attackers, these frogs have bright colors that announce their identity. Most predators recognize the colors as a warning and keep away.

The insect's front legs look like small leaves.

LEAF DISGUISE

Leaf insects of tropical forests are masters of camouflage. Their wings closely resemble leaves. The insects complete their disguise by positioning their bodies to match the tree they are resting on. Their disguise is so good that they are occasionally nibbled by leaf-eaters.

TREETOP HUNTER

Sharp-eyed harpy eagles are top predators of the Amazon rain forest. They use emergent trees as lookouts to survey the canopy and spot prey, such as monkeys, in the branches below. Then the eagle hurtles down at speeds of up to 50 mph (80 kph), snatching its victim in its sharp, hooked claws.

LURKING DANGER

The banks of South American rivers are the hunting ground of the caiman. It lurks in the murky water near the bank and pounces on animals that come to drink from the water's edge. Seizing prey with its snout, it pulls it into the water and holds it under until it drowns.

SPECTACULAR DISPLAY

Birds of paradise from Australasian rain forests are stunning birds. Males put on displays to show off their beautiful feathers to potential partners. The females are duller, so that they can hide in tree foliage while incubating eggs in the nest.

FINDING A MATE

DURING THE BREEDING SEASON, birds, mammals, and other creatures attract their partners through the dense rain forest foliage by using bright colors, loud calls, scents, or other signals. They may pair with just one mate or seek several partners. Most insects, fish, and reptiles produce large numbers of offspring as eggs, but then take little or no care of their babies. Birds and mammals use a different strategy, producing relatively few young, which they then feed and rear intensively. Some mammals stay in family groups, making it easier to find food and defend themselves.

INTENSIVE CARE

Mammals, and particularly primates such as this gibbon, invest more time rearing their young than any other animal. Mammal mothers feed their babies a nutritious diet of rich milk. A young gibbon grows up in a small family group with its mother, father, and older siblings. The baby stays with its family for at least two years, learning valuable survival skills from the older animals.

COURTING FROGS

Red-eyed tree frogs use sound to find their mates in the dark. The males utter loud croaking calls to signal to the females that they are strong and healthy, and so would make good mates. These tree frogs living high in the canopy descend to streams to lay their eggs, but do not look after their tadpoles.

The skin changes color from dark green to reddish-brown, depending on the frog's mood.

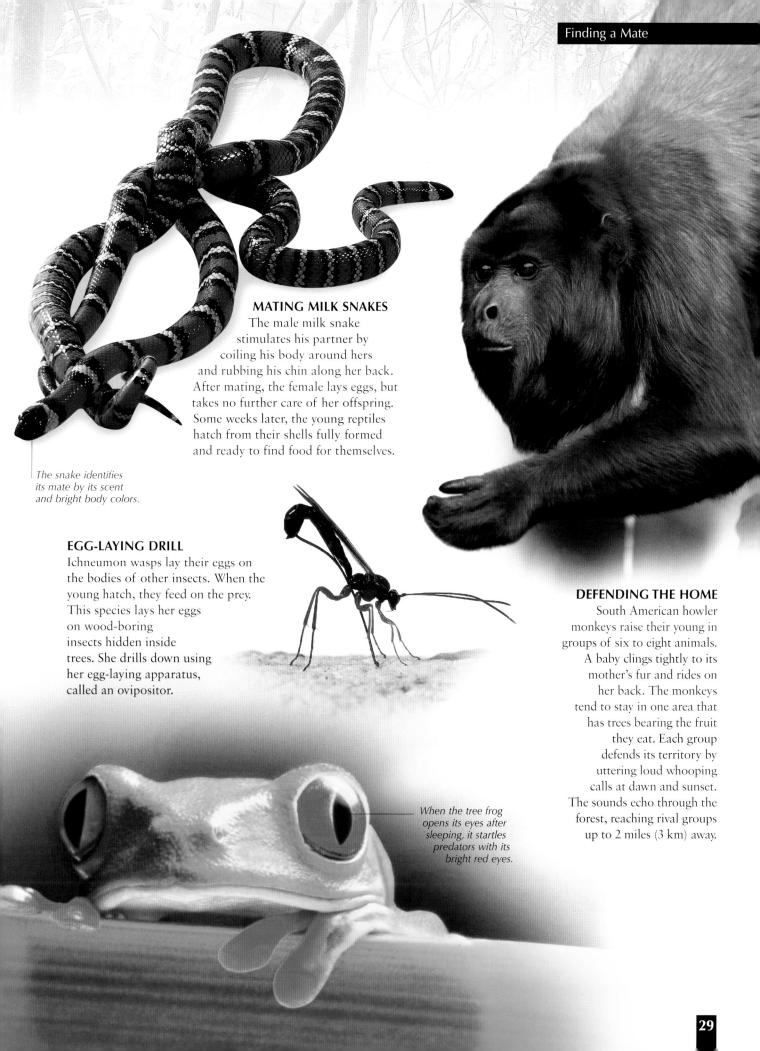

MATING MILK SNAKES

The male milk snake stimulates his partner by coiling his body around hers and rubbing his chin along her back. After mating, the female lays eggs, but takes no further care of her offspring. Some weeks later, the young reptiles hatch from their shells fully formed and ready to find food for themselves.

The snake identifies its mate by its scent and bright body colors.

EGG-LAYING DRILL

Ichneumon wasps lay their eggs on the bodies of other insects. When the young hatch, they feed on the prey. This species lays her eggs on wood-boring insects hidden inside trees. She drills down using her egg-laying apparatus, called an ovipositor.

When the tree frog opens its eyes after sleeping, it startles predators with its bright red eyes.

DEFENDING THE HOME

South American howler monkeys raise their young in groups of six to eight animals. A baby clings tightly to its mother's fur and rides on her back. The monkeys tend to stay in one area that has trees bearing the fruit they eat. Each group defends its territory by uttering loud whooping calls at dawn and sunset. The sounds echo through the forest, reaching rival groups up to 2 miles (3 km) away.

MOON MOTH

Madagascan Moon moths come out at night to feed on the nectar of night-opening flowers, which often release strong scents to attract insects. Eyespots on its wings may temporarily fool predators into believing that the moth is a large, dangerous creature such as an owl.

The wings of the Madagascan Moon moth can span up to 7 in (20 cm) in length.

FOREST AT NIGHT

R AIN FOREST ANIMALS can be divided into two main groups: diurnal creatures, which are active during daytime, and nocturnal animals, which search for food at night. This double shift means that fewer animals are out at any one time competing for food and shelter. As the sun sets, diurnal animals retire to rest, while the night shift awakes to go about its business. The senses of nocturnal animals are adapted to finding food in the dark. Bushbabies, tarsiers, and owls have large eyes that make the most of glimmers of light. Other animals, such as spiders and snakes, rely on excellent hearing, smell, touch, or other senses to find their food and, in the breeding season, to locate mates.

NIGHT-ADAPTED SENSES

Many snakes (like this tree boa) are nocturnal. As the boa lurks coiled in the canopy, its flickering tongue gathers scents in the air, which are then transferred to a scent organ in the roof of its mouth for identification. The boa also uses heat-sensitive pits on its lips to pinpoint warm-blooded prey.

Sensitive skin detects vibrations caused by animals moving in the canopy.

WANDERING SPIDER

The Central American rusty wandering spider hunts prey on the forest floor at night. Slit organs on its feet pick up vibrations caused by creatures rustling through the leaf litter. The spider pounces and injects its victim with a powerful poison.

LIGHT SIGNALS

At night, tropical forests glow with the tiny, winking lights of fireflies. These beetles use light to signal to their mates. Each species has its own pattern of flashes, like a private Morse code.

The firefly mixes two chemicals in an organ in its abdomen to make light.

USING ECHOLOCATION

Bats spend the day roosting upside down. They move around and hunt for prey at night using a natural sonar (navigation by sound) to avoid crashing into obstacles. They emit clicking noises, then react to the echoes that bounce back off solid objects.

KILLER INSTINCT

Bengal tigers hunt prey as large as deer, goats, and cattle. The striped coat breaks up the hunter's outline and conceals it in the shadows. Keen senses of smell and hearing help the tiger to locate prey, while a reflecting layer at the back of its eyes makes the most of any light.

BIG-EYED HUNTER

Southeast Asian tarsiers spend the day asleep on a branch. At dusk they hunt insects, and can eat about 40 prey in a single night. The large eyes see well in the gloom, and the long front fingers shoot out to snatch flying prey.

TEMPLE OF THE SUN

DEEP IN THE MIST-SHROUDED rain forest of Chiapas in Mexico lie the ruins of the ancient Mayan city of Palenque. The Mayan people lived in Central America from AD 250–900 and built magnificent palaces for their kings and pyramid-shaped temples to honor their gods. The Mayan king Chan-Bahlum built the Temple of the Sun in the seventh century to celebrate his accession to the throne. When the Mayans declined, their cities became overgrown by dense forest.

EXPLORING THE TEMPLE OF THE SUN

1 **Quetzal bird:** *sacred to the Mayan people, the quetzal's green feathers were used to adorn royal headdresses*

2 **Howler monkeys:** *the monkeys defend their territory by howling, a sound that carries a long distance*

3 **Monarch butterfly:** *fluttering high above the forest, the butterfly follows the same migration pattern every year*

4 **Elaborate headdress:** *the shaman wears a decorated headdress and performs a fire dance to the gods*

5 **Animal sacrifice:** *the Mayans made blood sacrifices to their gods, such as Chac, god of rain and lightning*

6 **Temple facade:** *walls were painted fiery reds and decorated with colorful pictures and hieroglyphs*

7 **Priest:** *during ceremonies, the priest prays to the gods for help, for example, for rain to grow crops*

8 **Burning braziers:** *as the sun sets, fires light the ceremony for the people watching from the foot of the steps*

FORESTS AND PEOPLE

THE WORLD'S RAIN FORESTS have always sustained people. Forest plants and animals provided food, medicine, clothing, and shelter for local peoples, as well as materials for tools and weapons. From the 15th century, Europeans arrived to explore and lay claim to remote tropical rain forests and harvest their resources. Now hundreds of forest products, from bananas, brazil nuts, avocados, pineapples, and cocoa for chocolate to herbs, spices, rubber, and even chewing gum, are widely cultivated and make their way to supermarket shelves around the world.

Statues of Aztec gods were created from molds and carved in stone.

The feathers have lost some of their color over the years.

FEATHER FAN
This fan, made from colorful macaw feathers, was made by the Incas, who ruled much of South America from about 1470 to 1532. Feathers were also used to make headdresses for religious ceremonies.

AZTEC GODDESS
After the Mayas, the Aztecs ruled Mexico until 1521. Like many forest peoples, they worshipped gods representing natural forces such as the Sun and rain. This statue shows Chicomecoatl, the goddess of ripe maize (the Aztec's staple food).

RAIN FOREST CITY
The moated city of Angkor in Cambodia was the capital of the Khmer Empire, which controlled much of Southeast Asia during the 12th and 13th centuries. The Khmer built many temples.

The Hindu temple of Angkor Wat has five bell-shaped towers.

FOREST DWELLING, ECUADOR

This longhouse is built from local materials such as lumber. Houses are often sited on rivers, which provide food and a means of transportation through dense forest. The houses are raised on stilts to prevent damage from floods.

The rosy periwinkle plant from Madagascar is used to treat leukemia, a type of cancer.

Calabar beans are used to treat glaucoma (a cause of blindness) and also to reduce high blood pressure.

Papaya fruits are used for infections caused by bacteria. Young plant stems can help to get rid of parasitic worms.

PLANT MEDICINE

The leaves, flowers, fruit, roots, and seeds of some forest plants contain medicinal chemicals that local people have known about for centuries. Calabar beans are highly poisonous when taken in large quantities, but a tiny amount can help to cure illnesses. The plants above are now used in Western medicine.

GUM HARVEST

This worker is cutting zigzag grooves in the bark of a chicle tree. The milky sap, called latex, that oozes from the cuts and flows down the tree is used to make chewing gum. Sap from chicle trees has been used for making gum since the time of the Mayas and Aztecs.

FARMING ON FOREST LAND

Large areas of forest are cleared to grow crops. However, farming exhausts the thin forest soil, so farmers clear a new patch. Intercropping—growing two crops side-by-side, like the cabbages and bananas here—helps to nourish the soil.

FRAGILE FORESTS

R AIN FORESTS ARE FRAGILE HABITATS, despite their great size and many wonders. More than 55,000 sq miles (140,000 sq km) of rain forests are felled each year. If the destruction continues, there will be hardly any forests left by 2050. Rain forest trees are cut down for lumber and fuel and to provide land for farming and mining. When trees are cut down, native plants and animals are threatened. Large-scale destruction can even affect the world's climate, since forests provide oxygen and recycle moisture. However, governments and groups in many areas are now taking steps to save the rain forests.

WOOD FOR FUEL

In many parts of the world, rain forest trees are felled to provide fuel for cooking. Some species of trees, such as this flame tree from the Cook Islands in Polynesia, are now rare, which also threatens the survival of forest creatures that depend on them.

RAIN FOREST RESERVE

The Monteverde Cloud Forest Reserve in Costa Rica is one of hundreds of reserves around the world that now protect wild rain forest land and the animals that live there. When tourists visit the reserve to enjoy the unspoiled forest, they pay a fee that helps to fund the park's upkeep, as well as local conservation projects. This type of tourism is known as ecotourism.

PLANTATIONS

This oil palm plantation in Borneo, Southeast Asia, occupies land that was once rain forest. Mature trees secure the soil in wet, hilly areas like this. When they are removed erosion of the land can become a problem. The slopes on this plantation have been terraced in an effort to stop the soil from washing away.

LOGGING

Tropical trees such as teak and mahogany yield lumber called hardwood—tough, fine-grained wood that is used to make beautiful furniture. So many of these mighty trees have been felled that they are now scarce. In some places, logging tropical hardwoods is now forbidden, but it still goes on illegally.

REPLANTING THE FOREST

In sustainable forestry projects like this one in Asia, young tree seedlings are planted to replace mature trees that have been felled. However, hardwood trees are very slow-growing, so it will be many years before these young trees are ready to be harvested.

SAVING FOREST LIFE

Forest creatures endangered by habitat destruction include Madagascan lemurs, and these orangutans from Borneo. These large forest apes now live in a sanctuary where they are looked after until they are ready to be released back into the wild.

INDEX

ACKNOWLEDGMENTS

Dorling Kindersley would like to thank Dorothy Frame for the index and Margaret Parrish for proof reading.

The publisher would like to thank the following for their kind permission to reproduce their photographs:
(Key: a=above; c=center; b=below; l=left; r=right; t=top; Ace=acetate)
Alamy Images: Sue Cunningham 32Ace cl (foliage); Robert Harding World Imagery 37b; Malie Rich-Griffith 29tr; Tom Till 15tl.
Ardea.com: Jean-Paul Ferrero 19tl, 19cl, 37cr; Francois Gohier 7cla; John Mason 10bc, 11Ace cbl (ants), 16-17 (midges); P. Morris 23Ace crb (fish); M. Watson 32cal; Jim Zipp 32clb (heron). **Bruce Coleman Ltd.:** Luiz Claudio Marigo 22Ace cla (uakari). **Corbis:** Dave Bartruff 10Ace tl; Tom Brakefield 31bl; Macduff Everton 32&Ace (temple); Gallo Images 35cl; Wolfgang Kaehler 35tl; David Muench 32cr, 32cal-32Ace (hanging foliage); Galen Rowell 32bcl-32Ace bcr (treetops); Chase Swift 5cr, 28-29b; Craig Tuttle 32-33&Ace(sky). **DK Images:** Alan Watson 7tr, 22-23&Ace (mossy vines), 32cbl; American Museum of Natural History 35cb; INAH Mexico/Michael Zabé 34tl; Natural History Museum 30tl; Royal Museum of Scotland 34cr; Jerry Young 21cla, 27cl, 28tr. **Michael and Patricia Fogden:** 10Ace cb (fungus), 11cb. **FLPA:** Derek L. Hall 33Ace cl; Frank W. Lane 32Ace ca (leaf), 32bl (bird & leaf), 32car; Frans Lanting/Minden 18bl, 37tl;

Chris Mattison 12tr; Flip Nicklen/Minden 23cr; Fritz Polking 19cbl; Tui de Roy/Minden 27tr.
Getty Images: Grant Faint 5bl, 34b, 36br; Tim Flach 31tr; Joseph Van Os 5cl, 15br. **Justin Kerr** 33Ace cbl, 33cbr. **Lonely Planet Images:** Luke Hunter 36bl. **Nature Picture Library Ltd.:** Ingo Arndt 20tl; Martin Dohrn 10bl; Pete Oxford 25tr, 27tl; Doug Wechsler 25b. **National Geographic Image Collection:** Steve Winter 7bl; Paul Zahl 23Ace c. **N.H.P.A.:** George Bernard 21tr; Mark Bowler 21cl, 22 Ace b 23Ace bl; James Carmichael Jr. 22bcl (spider); Stephen Dalton 8tl, 16car (blowfly), 22Ace br, 22Ace c, 22Ace ca (macaws), 26bl, 32Ace cbl, 32Ace crb; Nick Garbutt 25cl; Martin Harvey 21br, 32br; Adrian Hepworth 30br; Daniel Heuclin 27br; Jean-Louis le Moigne 22cra (cacique bird); Eric Soder 9tr.

Oxford Scientific Films: John Brown 11Ace clb (ants); Carol Farneti Foster 20bc; Michael Fogden 24b; Peter Gathercole 23Ace bcr; Brian Kenney 11Ace cl (tarantula); Alan Root/SAL 10Ace cla; Tony Tilford 28tl. **Photonirvana.com/Alex Robinson:** 33br, 33Ace cbl. **Science Photo Library:** Gregory Dimijian 14br; Fletcher & Baylis 19tr; Simon Fraser 6bl; Jeff Lepore 9tl; Tom McHugh 12c, 31br; David Nunuk 37cl; Gregory Ochocki 23cb; Dr. Morley Read 5tr, 9bl, 13cl, 18br; Helen Williams 20cl. **South American Pictures:** Chris Sharp 35r. **Still Pictures:** Mark Edwards 36tl; Edward Parker 22Ace cbl (uakari); J. Rey-Millet 22cl (jaguar); Roland Seitre 23cla (uakari). **Werner Forman Archive:** Private Collection, New York 33Ace c (incense burner).
All other images © Dorling Kindersley www.dkimages.com